How to use the patterns in this book?

The patterns in this book are ready to use with single side printed pages so you can easily cut out the page and paste it on a suitable piece of wood.

Of course, you can photocopy, scale and alter the patterns according to your convenience.

Some patterns have details that might be challenging to cut on a smaller scale, so we recommend using paint to add the tiny details.

Some projects might be easy to do but most projects probably will be challenging for any beginner.

The outcome of the project will depend on your choice of materials and how far can you challenge your creativity and skills.

Safety: When working with any tools or wood, safety is a priority. Please, ensure you adhere to all the safety measures and wearing all the suitable protective equipment. Your own safety is your own responsibility.

Some tools you might need:

1- Your choice of wood to cut out the patterns, you can mix different wood types and colors for each layer of the patterns, the limit is your creativity and willingness to challenge your skills.
2- Scroll saw and suitable good blades.
3- Adhesive spray or glue to paste the patterns on the wood.
4- Frame with grooves to make the layered shadow box, or you can just glue the panels on top of each other and create a layered art (general instructions can be found below).
5- Light string or stripe (optional).
6- Paint and brush (optional).
7- Sandpaper.
8- Measuring tape.

Putting the patterns on the wood

There are many ways to transfer the patterns to the wood from drawing to using carbon paper or using spray adhesives. One of the common and effective ways is to add painter tape to cover the face of the wood then spray the adhesive spray and paste the paper pattern above the painter tape.

The painter tape function is to make it easier to remove the pattern after cutting without leaving any glue residue.

Another popular method is to directly paste the pattern on the wood with the spray adhesive and then after cutting, the pattern can be removed with the help of adhesive removal or mineral spirits.

Some basic tips, you probably knew

1- Safety is your primary priority.

2- Learning to use a scroll saw is like learning how to drive a manual car, no one is good at driving from their first try.

3- Woodworking is rewarding but needs patience, decision making and fixing mistakes.

4- When using a scroll saw, always start with cutting the inner details first. Some patterns in this book have details that might be challenging to cut on a smaller scale, so we recommend using paint to add these tiny details.

5- Make sure that your table saw blade is aligned with the miter slot and that the blade is squared or at 90 degrees.

6- Decide the plate entry holes for each part of the patterns.

7- During cutting, take care of the blade drift that might happen.

8- Finishing the project by sanding and painting the wood is recommended to make the project more interesting.

9- Have fun and enjoy!

There are two options for the end product;

The first option: cut out all the layers and glue them directly on top of each other to create a 3d layered art without any frame or light source.

Second option: build a shadow box frame with spaced grooves in the frame walls (the

number of grooves is equal to the number of the project's layers). The cutout layers or panels can then be fitted inside the grooves of the frame.
If you'd like to add light, then you can drill some holes on the inside layers to weave the light string through between the layers so that each layer has light in the space behind it. That will create a beautiful effect, and the shadow box can be used as a night light.
If a picture is worth a thousand words, then a video is worth a billion words. So, we highly recommend searching the web for videos on how to build a lighted 3d shadow box with a scroll saw. There are some short videos that you might find very useful.

For a lighted 3d shadow box there are three main components

1- Frame (instructions to build the frame can be found below).
2- Cutout Layers from the patterns or the panels.
3- Light source e.g. LED light string or strip, one color or multicolored, battery-operated or corded, the choice is yours.

How can you build the frame for the shadow box?

The following instructions are basic guidance and for sure, there are many other ways to build a frame.
Because building a frame requires some tools, please remember safety is your responsibility.
1- First decide the space you want to leave between layers.
2- Knowing the spacing and number of the layers as well as the thickness of each layer, you can then calculate the depth of the frame for your project.
3- Calculate the length of the frame sides e.g. most of the patterns are 7.5x7.5 inches so the total length of the wood strip needed for that frame will be 30 inches.
4- Cut the desired length and width of wood to make the frame.
5- Measure and mark the width and positions of the grooves.
6- Make the grooves with a dodo blade or router or table saw blade or even with hand tools.
7- Cut the long wood stripe into the four sides of the frame.

8- Using a tiled table saw at 45 degrees and cut mitered ends on four pieces so that it is easy to assemble the frame.

9- Now it is the time to add the final touches on the frame sides, either to sand or paint.

10- Glue three sides together on the mitered ends, leaving the fourth side open to slide in the panels.

11- Add the finished and painted bottom layer, if you will add light string, now it's the time to attach it and decide where it will be.

12- If you use a battery-operated light, it is a good idea to build a battery support box that is attached to the back of the bottom layer. It is simply a frame for the battery box, with three sides aligned with the battery box, leaving one side open for the battery box to slide in and out, in case of battery replacement. To secure the battery box, a fourth piece of wood could be added on top of the battery box.

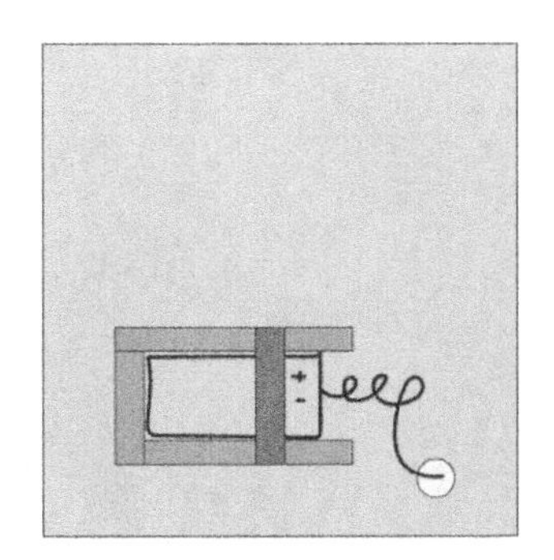

If you use a corded light, then a small hole to let the cord out is what is needed.

13- Decide where you are going to attach the light string, are you going to make it only on the background or also in between the layers/panels?

If you decide to weave the light in between the layers, make sure to make the holes on alternating sides so that it is easy to pass or weave the light string.

You might use hot glue to secure the light string in its place.

14- Add all the finished layers and light string, make sure everything is working as you want before closing the frame and gluing the last side of the frame.

15- Have fun and enjoy!

Content

<table>
<tr>
<td>Wolf (5 layers)
Size: 7.5 x 7.5 inches or 19x19 cm
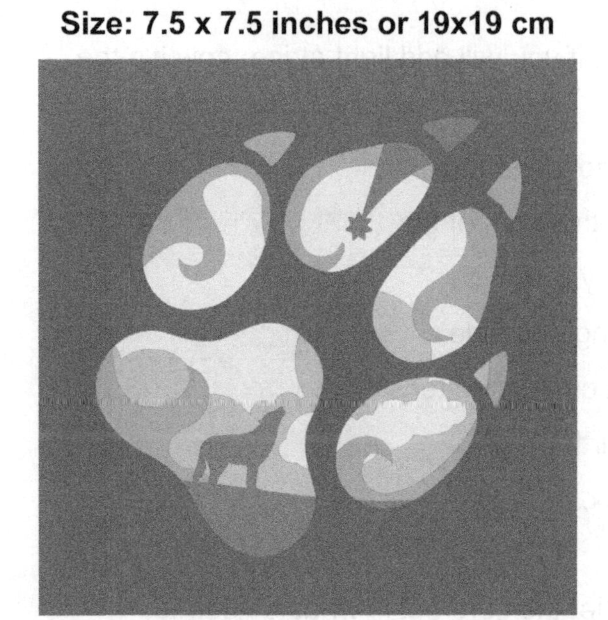</td>
<td>Bear (4 layers)
Size: 7.5 x 7.5 inches or 19x19 cm
</td>
</tr>
<tr>
<td>Birds (3 layers)
Size: 7.5 x 7.5 inches or 19x19 cm
</td>
<td>Cactus in the desert (5 layers)
Size: 7.5 x 7.5 inches or 19x19 cm
</td>
</tr>
</table>

Flamingo (5 layers)

Size: 7.5 x 7.5 inches or 19x19 cm

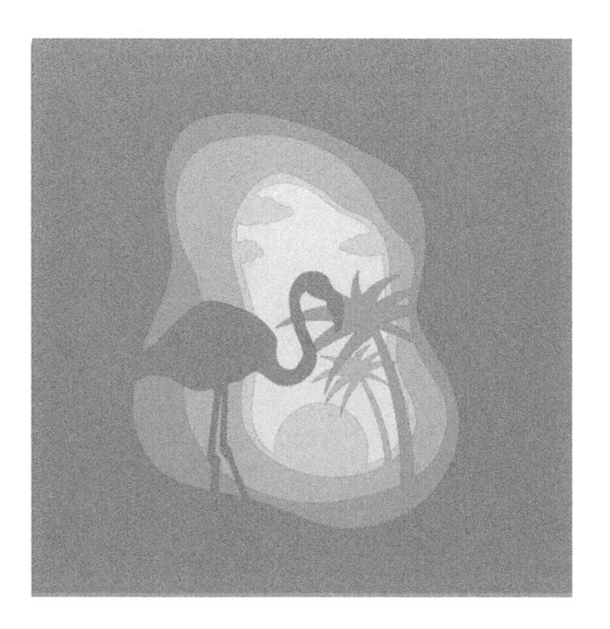

Beach (4 layers)

Size: 7.5 x 7.5 inches or 19x19 cm

Heart & Plane (4 layers)

Size: 7.5 x 7.5 inches or 19x19 cm

Paris (6 layers)

Size 7.5 x7.5 inch or 19x19 cm

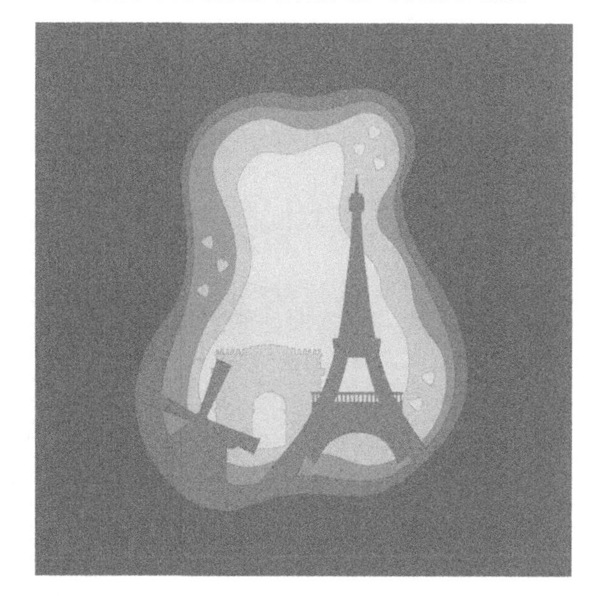

Venice (6 layers) **Size: 7.5 x7.5 inch or 19x19 cm** 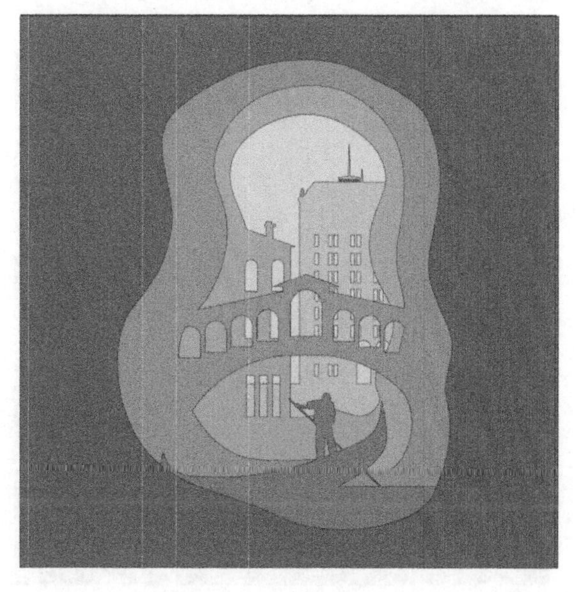	**Wild horse (4 layers)** **Size: 7.5 x 7.5 inches or 19x19 cm** 
Light house (4 layers) **Size: 7.5 x 7.5 inches or 19x19 cm** 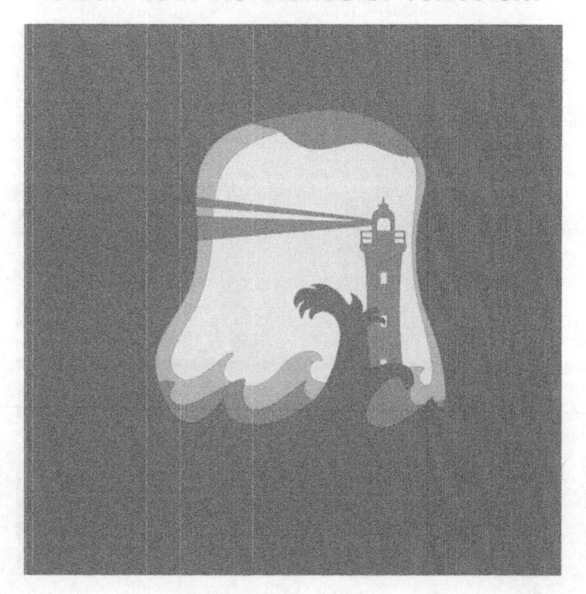	**Ocean (6 layers)** **Size: 7.5 x 7.5 inches or 19x19 cm** 

Deer in the forest (4 layers) Size 7.5 x7.5 inch or 19x19 cm 	House in the forest (4 layers) Size: 7.25 inches x 9 inches or 18.41 cm x 23 cm 
Nature scene (7 layers) Size: 7.25 inches x 9 inches or 18.41 cm x 23 cm 	Hiking (4 layers) Size: 7.25 inches x 9 inches or 18.41 cm x 23 cm 

Mermaid (5 layers) **Size: 7.25 inches x 9 inches or 18.41 cm x 23 cm** 	**Cowboy (4 layers)** **Size: 7.25 inches x 10 inches or 18.41 cm x 25.4 cm** 
Safari (5 layers) **Size: 7.25 inches x 10 inches or 18.41 cm x 25.4 cm** 	**Swan (5 layers)** **Size: 7 inches x 10 inches or 17.78 cm x 25.4 cm** 

Wolf (5 layers)

Size: 7.5 x 7.5 inches or 19x19 cm

This Page is Intentionally Left blank.

Wolf Layer 1 (Bottom)

This Page is Intentionally Left blank.

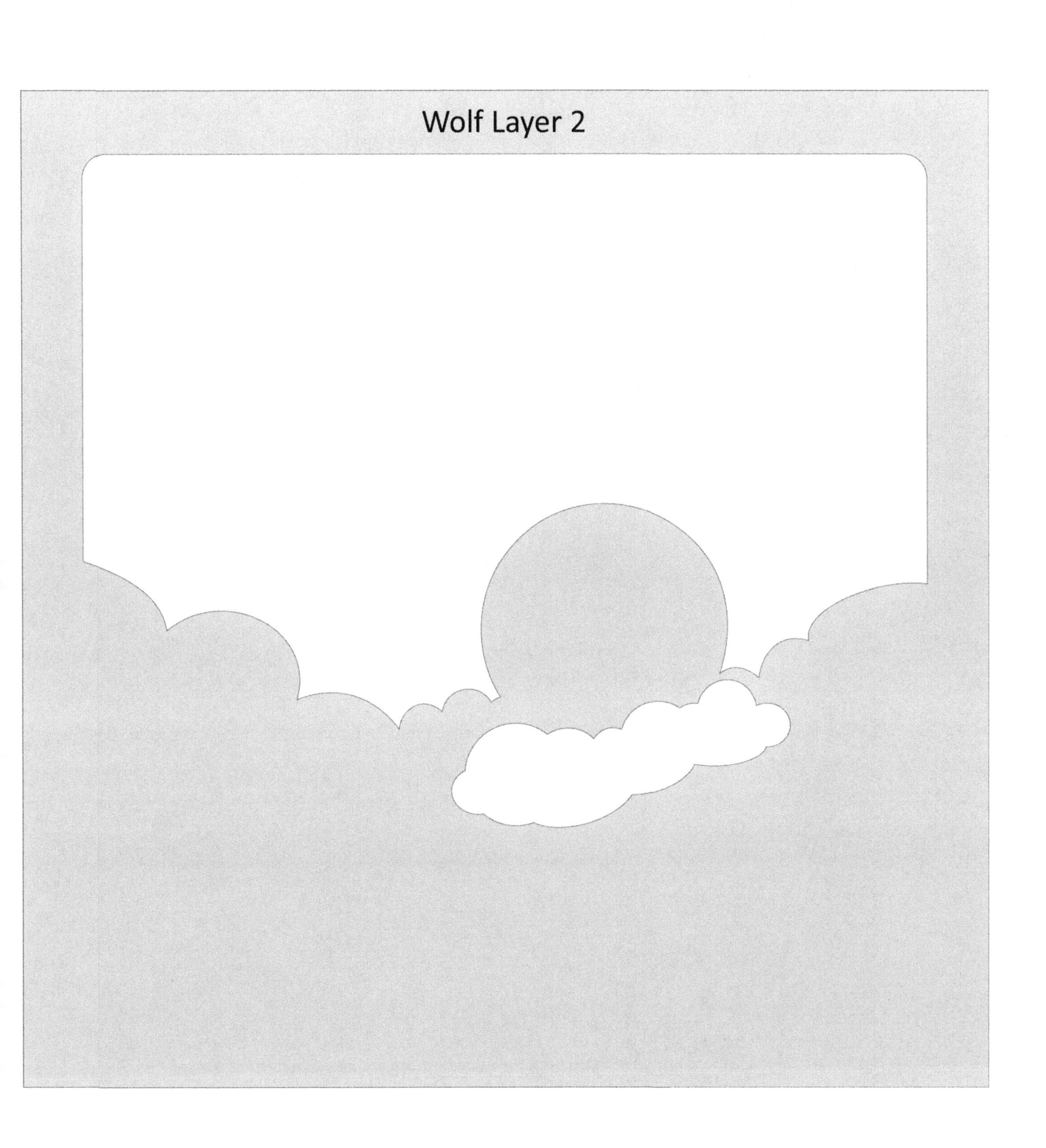
Wolf Layer 2

This Page is Intentionally Left blank.

Wolf Layer 3

This Page is Intentionally Left blank.

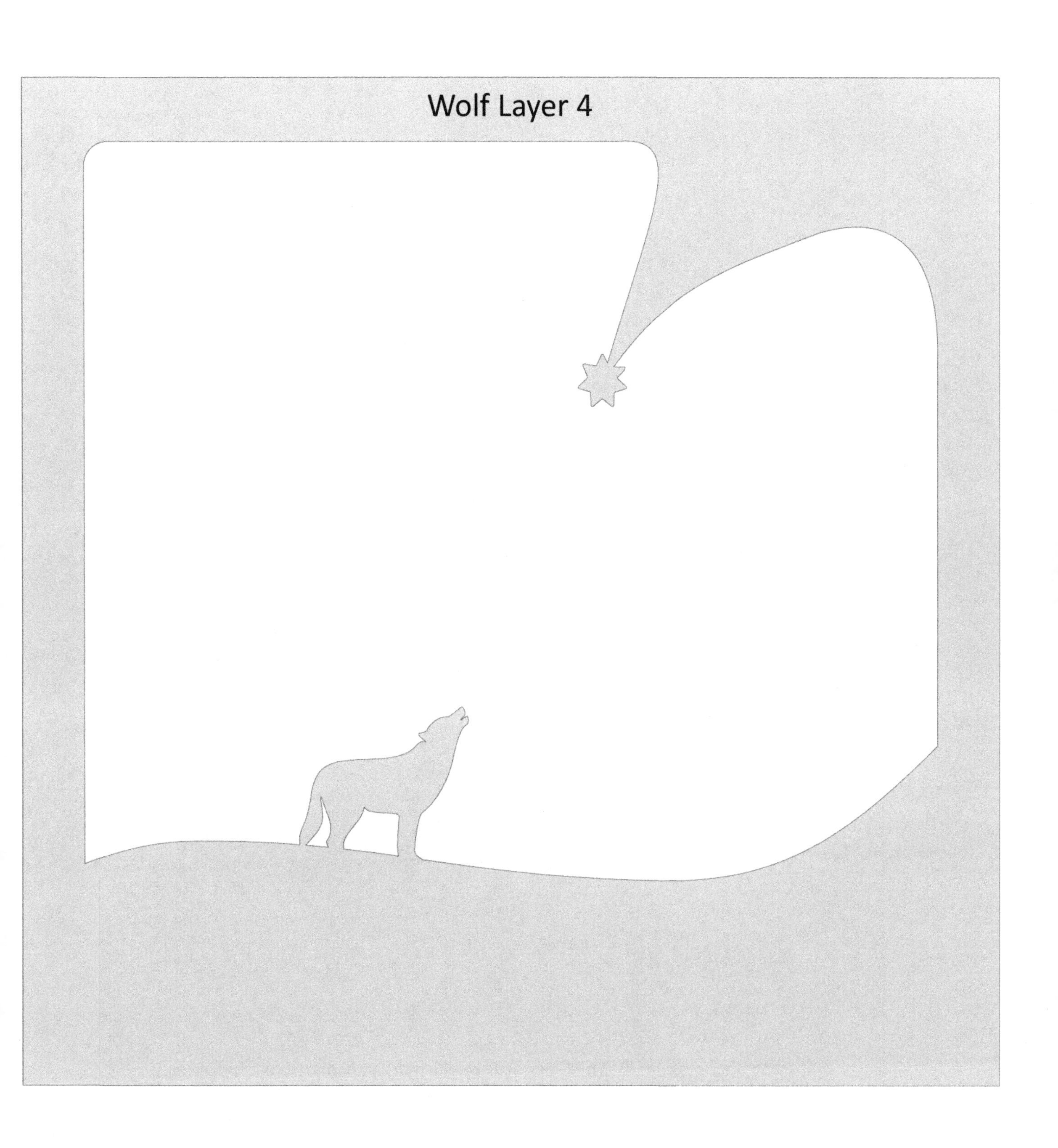
Wolf Layer 4

This Page is Intentionally Left blank.

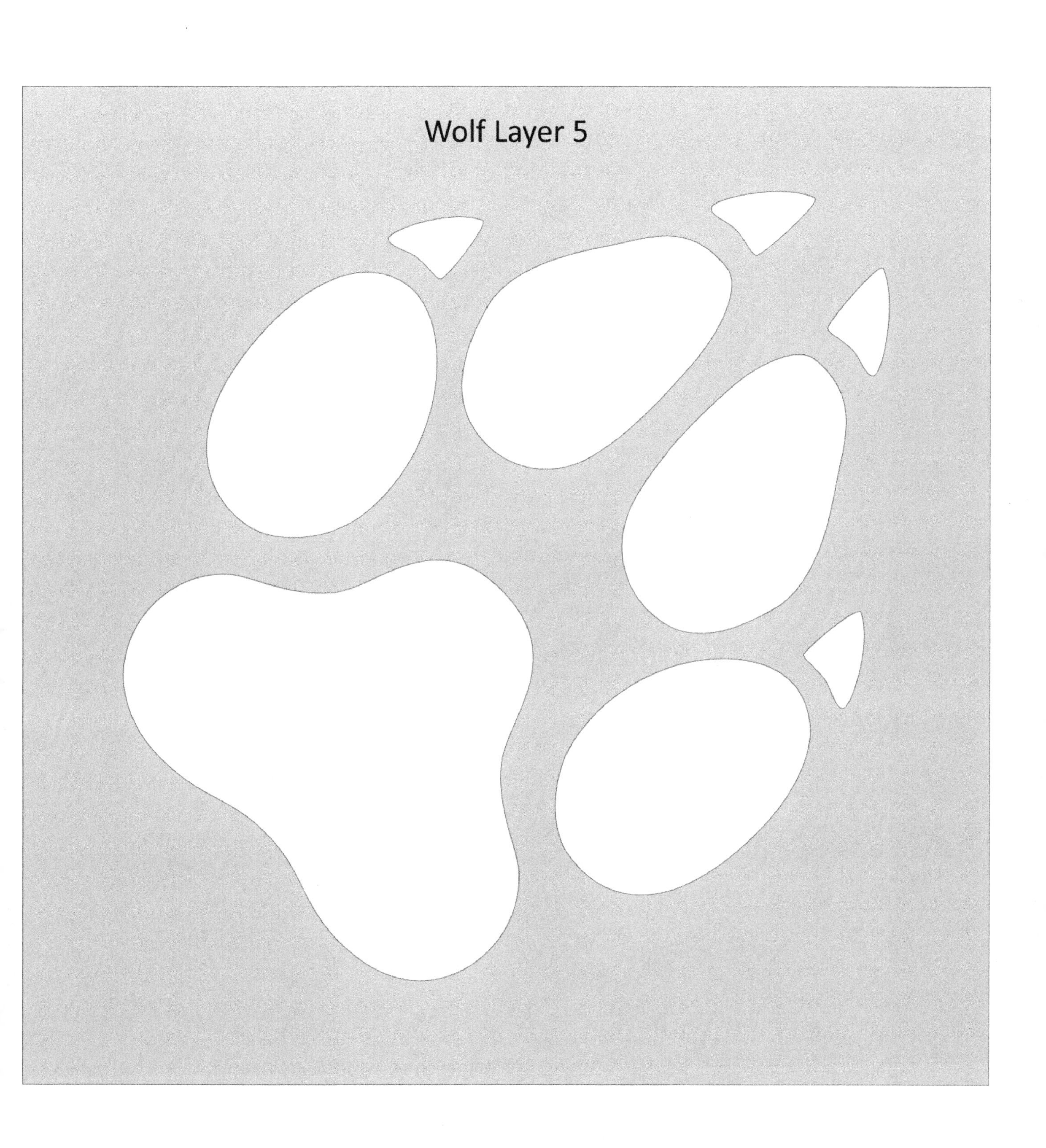
Wolf Layer 5

This Page is Intentionally Left blank.

Bear (4 layers)

Size: 7.5 x 7.5 inches or 19x19 cm

This Page is Intentionally Left blank.

Bear Layer 1

This Page is Intentionally Left blank.

Bear Layer 2

This Page is Intentionally Left blank.

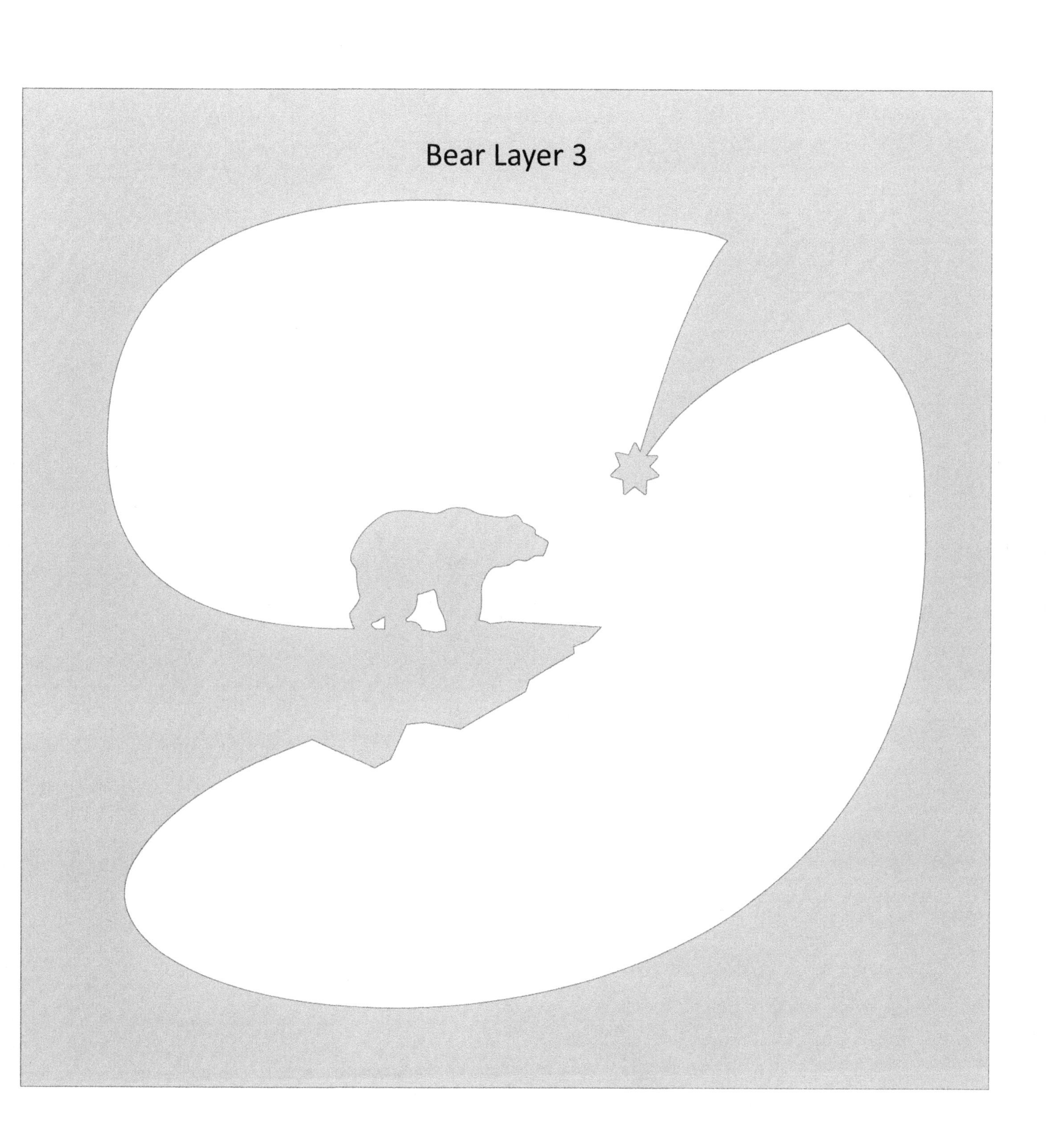
Bear Layer 3

This Page is Intentionally Left blank.

Bear Layer 4

This Page is Intentionally Left blank.

Birds (3 layers)

Size: 7.5 x 7.5 inches or 19x19 cm

This Page is Intentionally Left blank.

Birds Layer 1

This Page is Intentionally Left blank.

Birds Layer 2

This Page is Intentionally Left blank.

Birds Layer 3

This Page is Intentionally Left blank.

Cactus in the desert (5 layers)

Size: 7.5 x 7.5 inches or 19x19 cm

This Page is Intentionally Left blank.

Cactus Layer 1

This Page is Intentionally Left blank.

Cactus Layer 2

This Page is Intentionally Left blank.

Cactus Layer 3

This Page is Intentionally Left blank.

Cactus Layer 4

This Page is Intentionally Left blank.

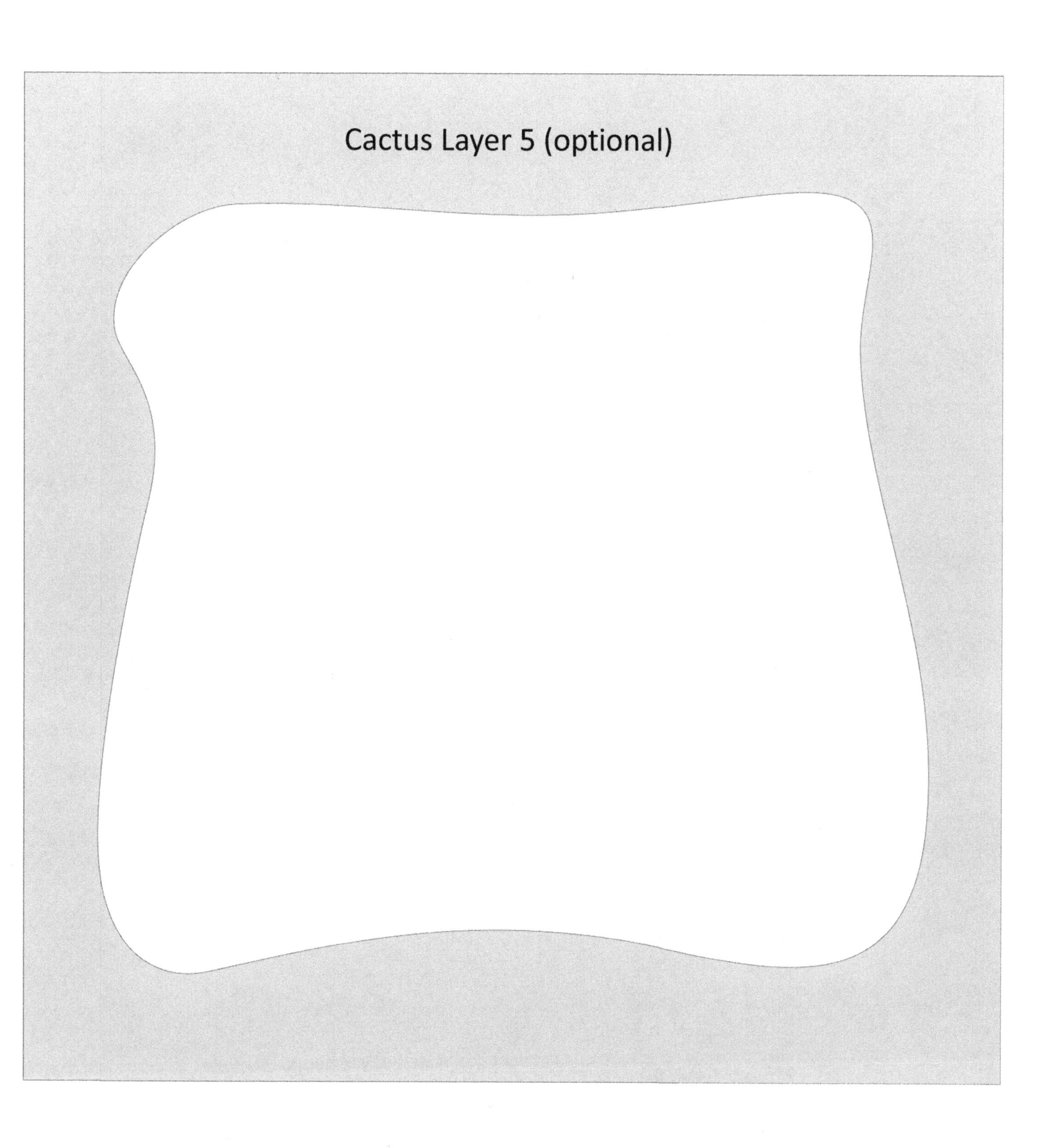
Cactus Layer 5 (optional)

This Page is Intentionally Left blank.

Flamingo (5 layers)

Size: 7.5 x 7.5 inches or 19x19 cm

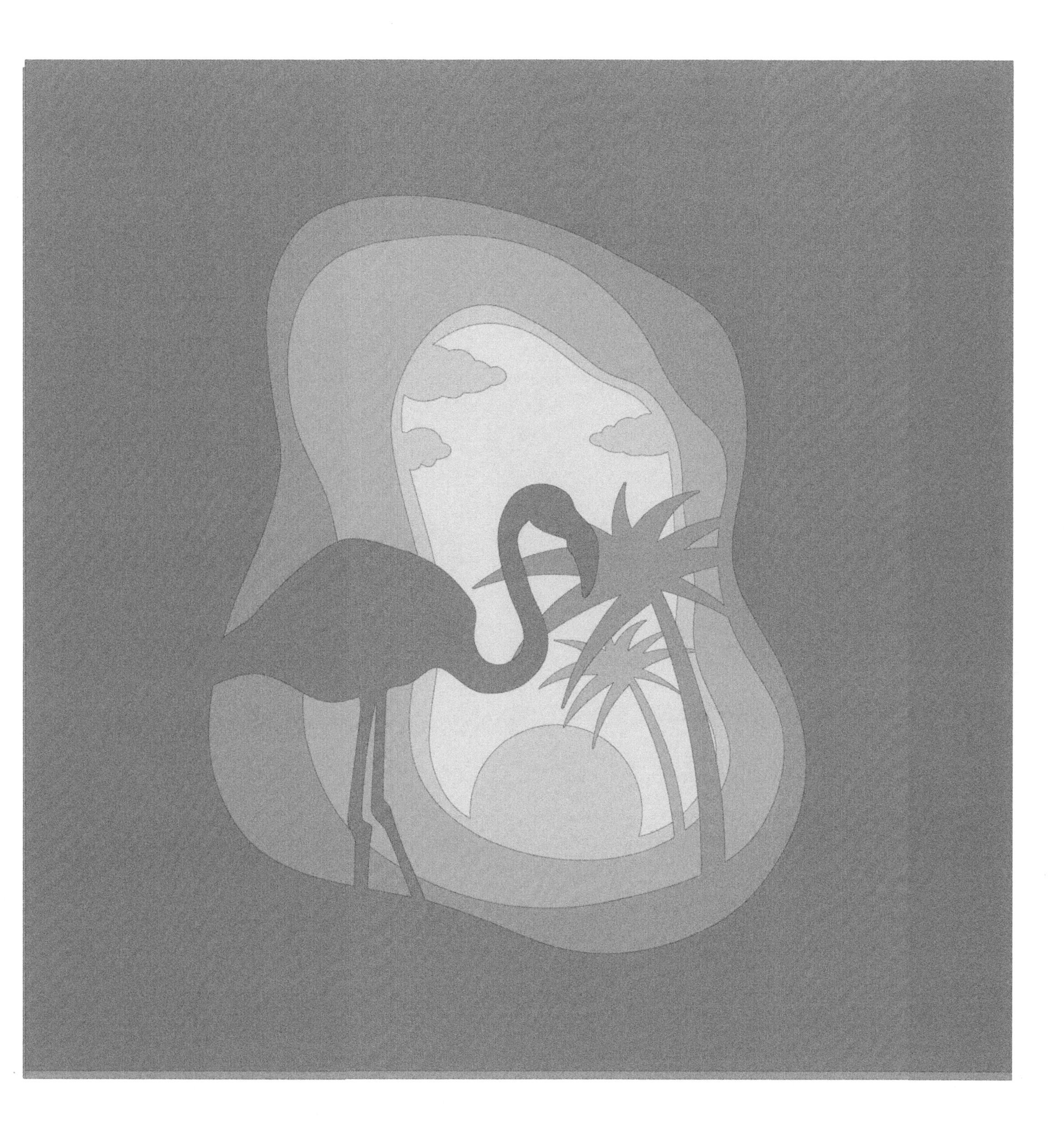

This Page is Intentionally Left blank.

Flamingo Layer 1

This Page is Intentionally Left blank.

Flamingo Layer 2

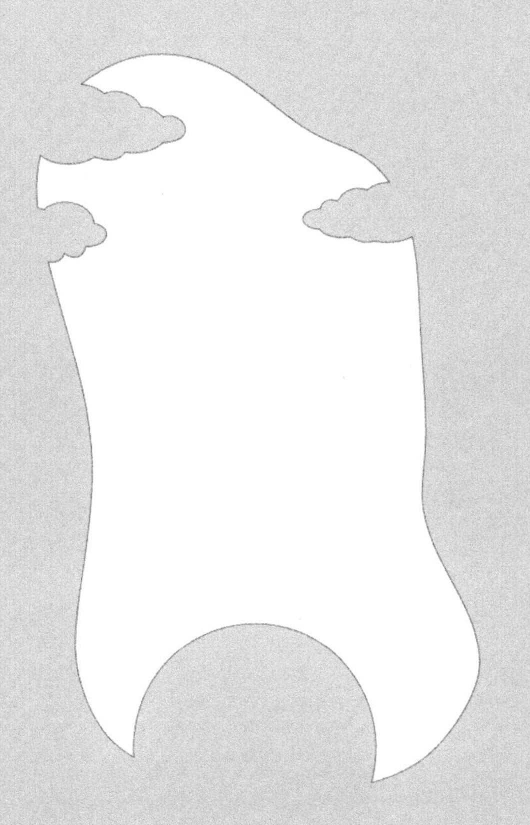

This Page is Intentionally Left blank.

Flamingo Layer 3

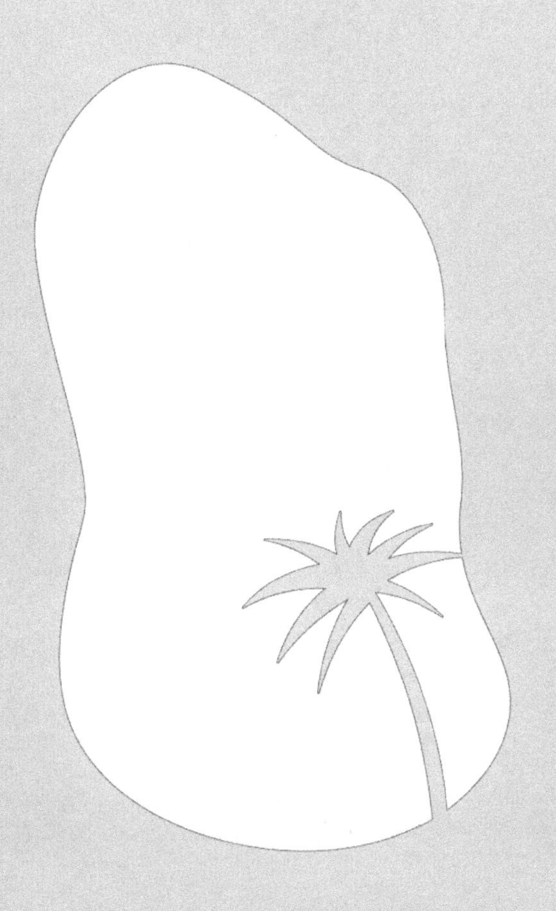

This Page is Intentionally Left blank.

Flamingo Layer 4

This Page is Intentionally Left blank.

Flamingo Layer 5

This Page is Intentionally Left blank.

Beach (4 layers)

Size: 7.5 x 7.5 inches or 19x19 cm

This Page is Intentionally Left blank.

Beach Layer 1

This Page is Intentionally Left blank.

Beach Layer 2

This Page is Intentionally Left blank.

Beach Layer 3

This Page is Intentionally Left blank.

Beach Layer 4

This Page is Intentionally Left blank.

Heart & Plane (4 layers)

Size: 7.5 x 7.5 inches or 19x19 cm

This Page is Intentionally Left blank.

Heart & Plane Layer 1

This Page is Intentionally Left blank.

Heart & Plane Layer 2

This Page is Intentionally Left blank.

The Details of the mountain are optional to cut out or to paint

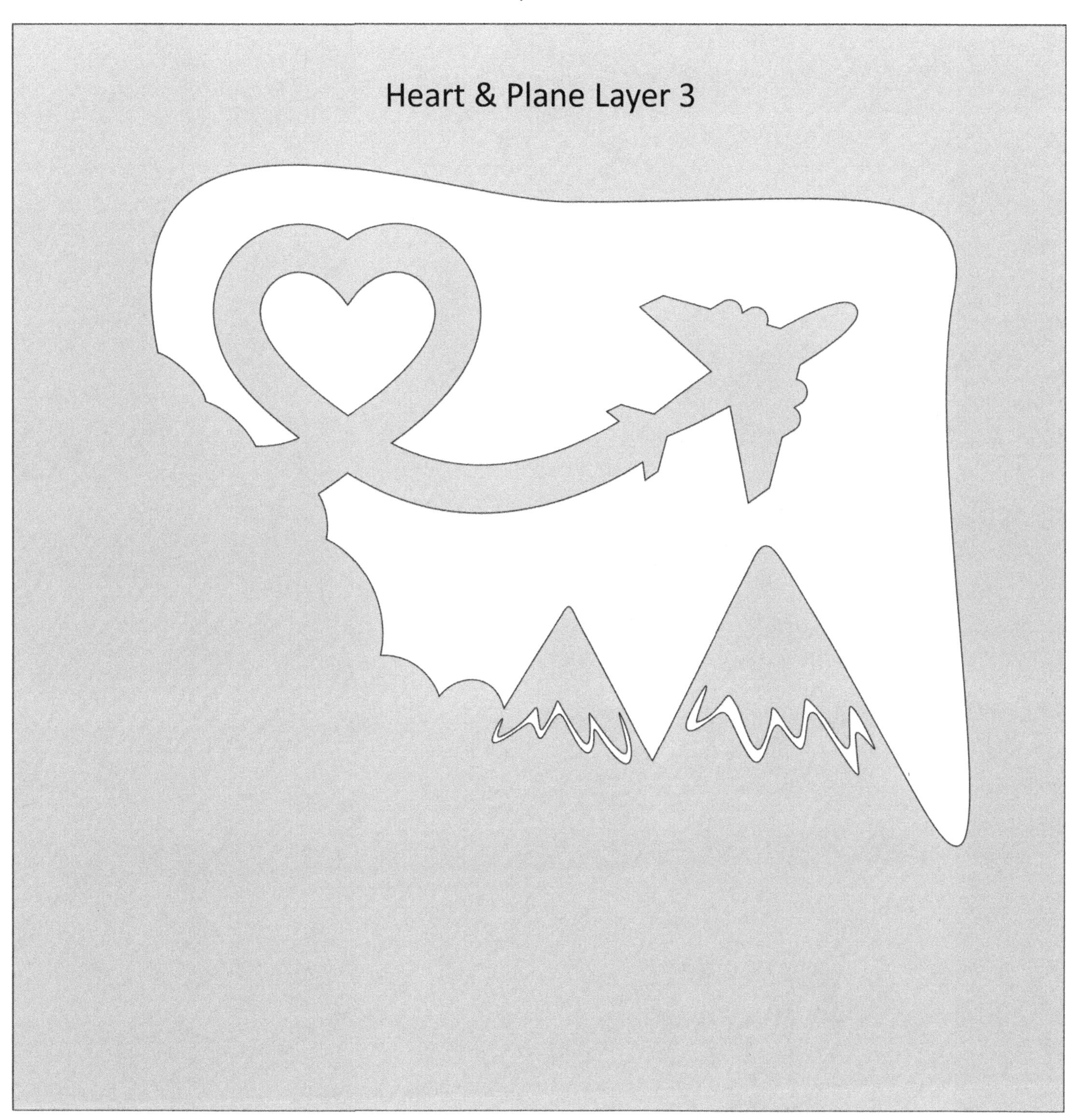

This Page is Intentionally Left blank.

Heart & Plane Layer 4

This Page is Intentionally Left blank.

Paris (6 layers)

Size 7.5 x7.5 inch or 19x19 cm

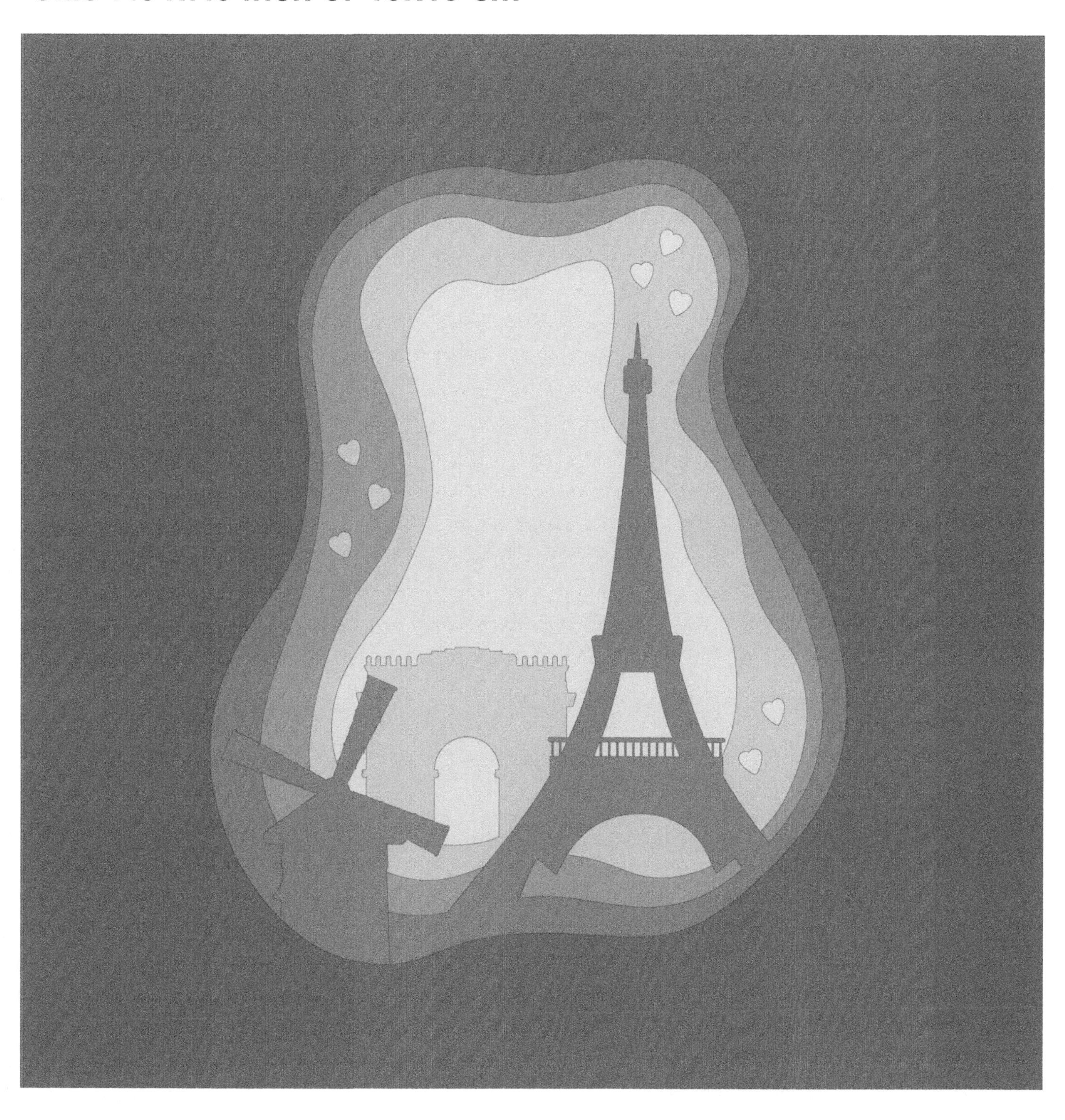

This Page is Intentionally Left blank.

Paris Layer 1

This Page is Intentionally Left blank.

Paris Layer 2

This Page is Intentionally Left blank.

Paris Layer 3

This Page is Intentionally Left blank.

The Details of the Eiffel tower are for painting guide.

This Page is Intentionally Left blank.

Paris Layer 5

This Page is Intentionally Left blank.

Paris Layer 6

This Page is Intentionally Left blank.

Venice (6 layers)

Size: 7.5 x7.5 inch or 19x19 cm

This Page is Intentionally Left blank.

Venice Layer 1

This Page is Intentionally Left blank.

The Details of the light and the light house are optional to cut out or to paint

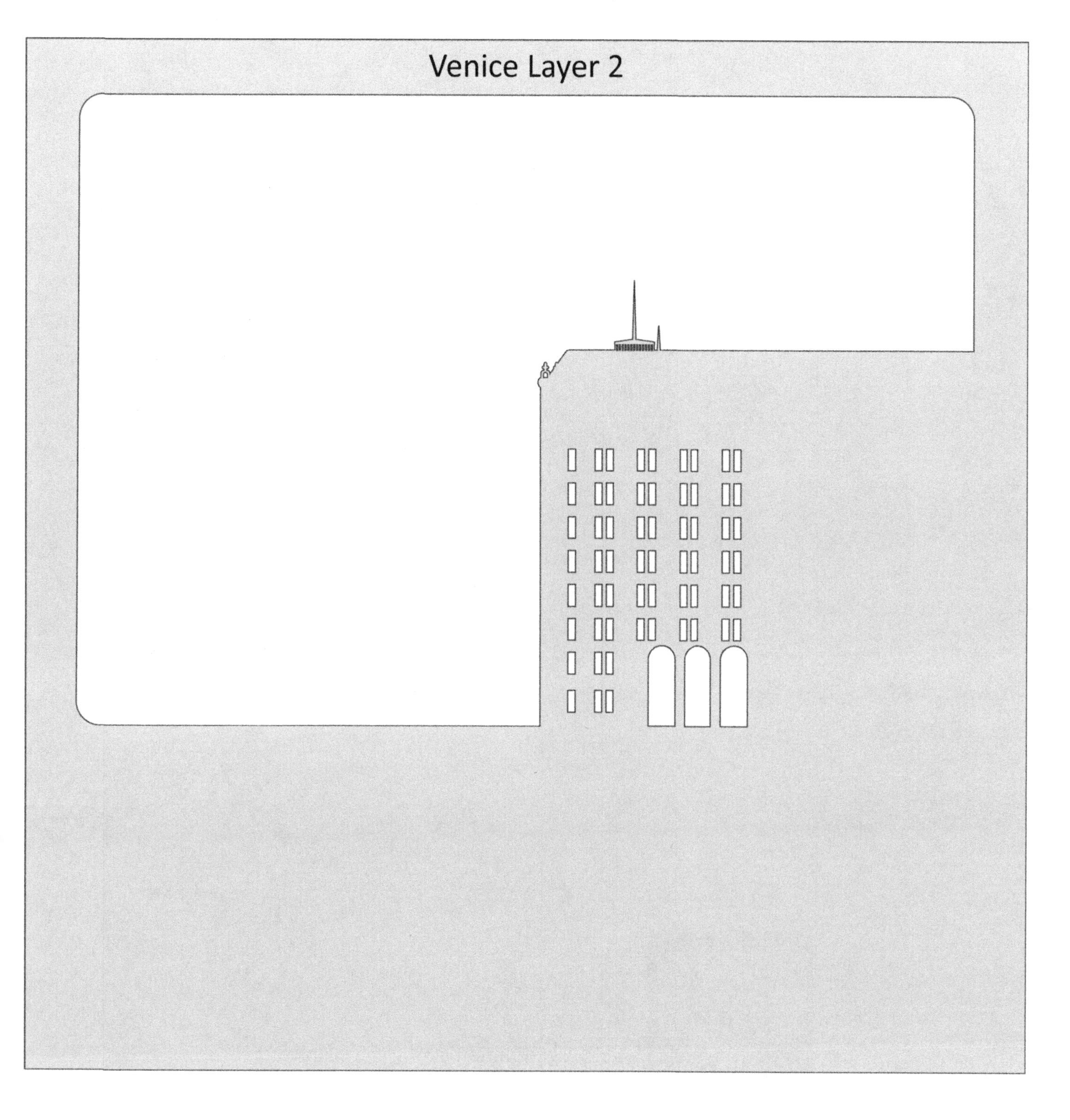

This Page is Intentionally Left blank.

Venice Layer 3

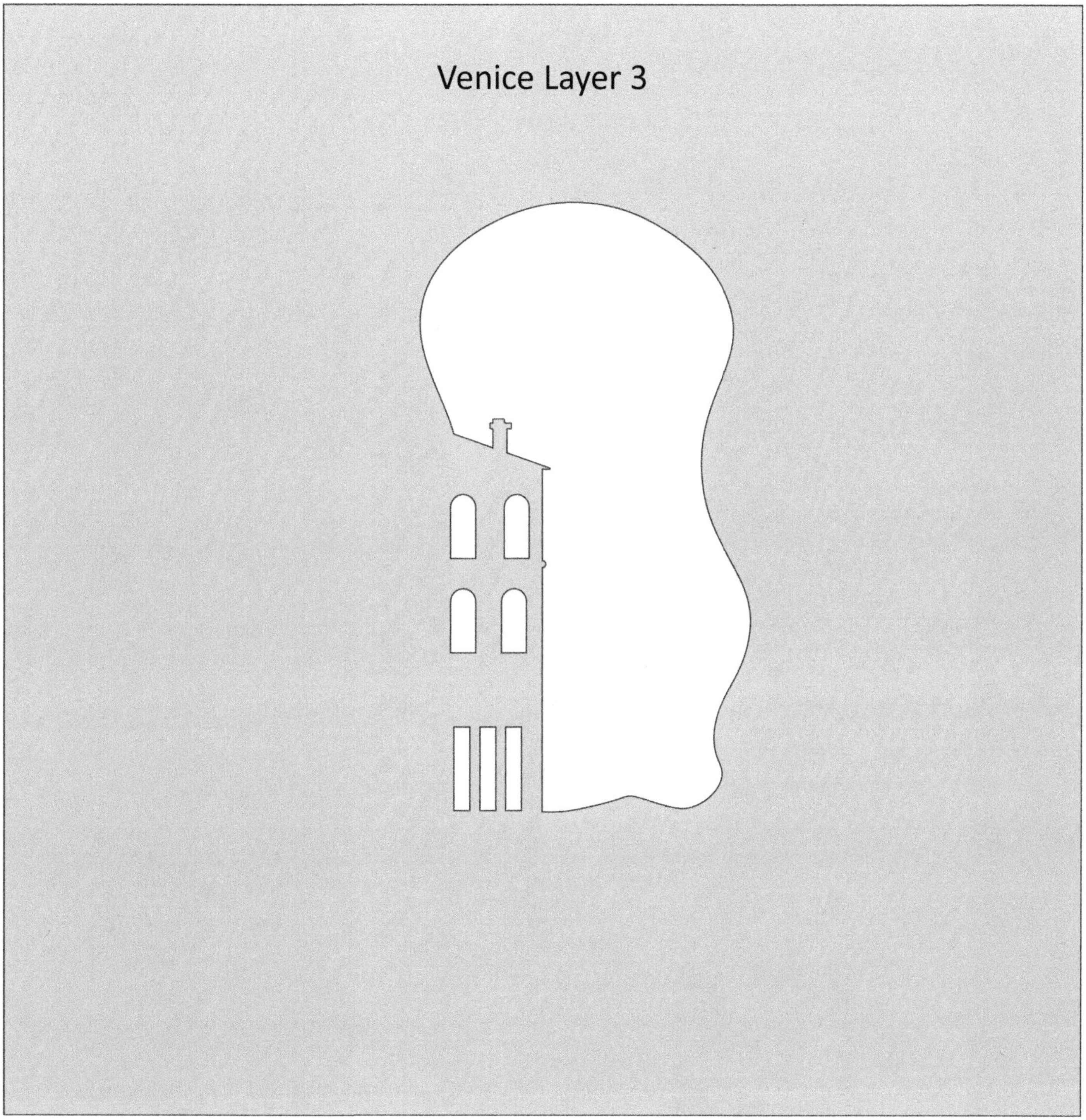

This Page is Intentionally Left blank.

Venice Layer 4

This Page is Intentionally Left blank.

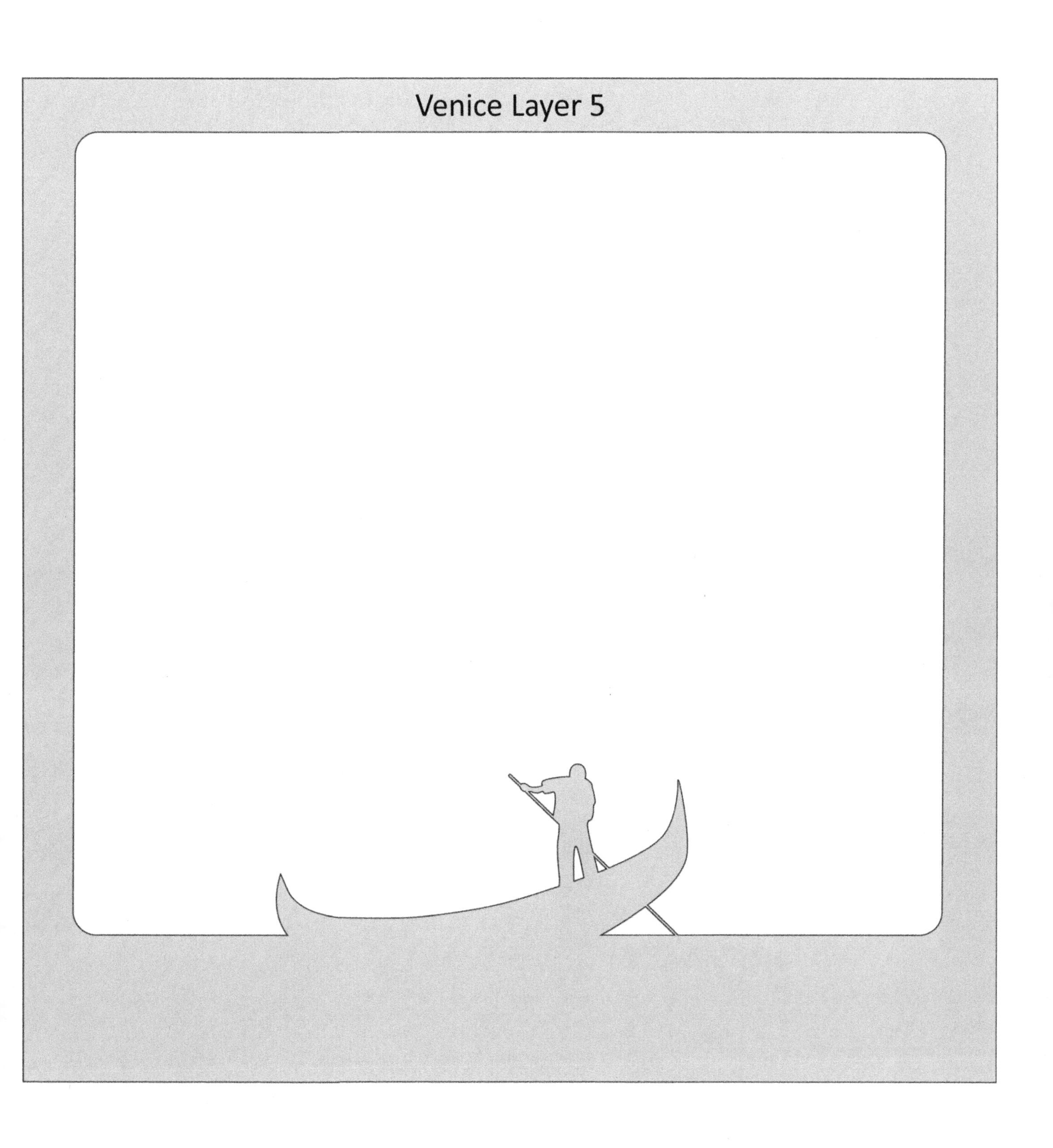
Venice Layer 5

This Page is Intentionally Left blank.

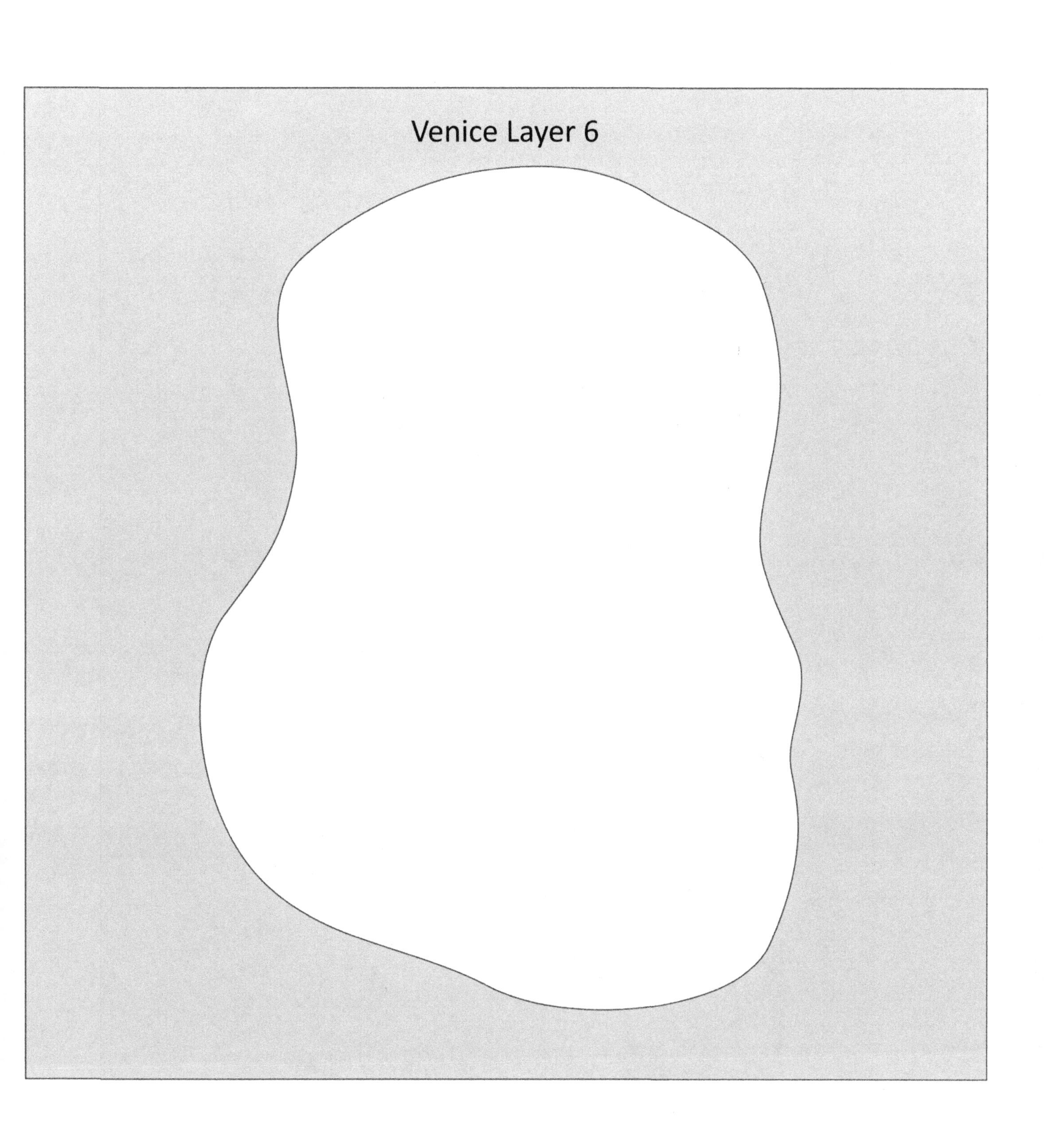
Venice Layer 6

This Page is Intentionally Left blank.

Wild horse (4 layers)

Size: 7.5 x 7.5 inches or 19x19 cm

This Page is Intentionally Left blank.

The Details are optional to cut out or to paint

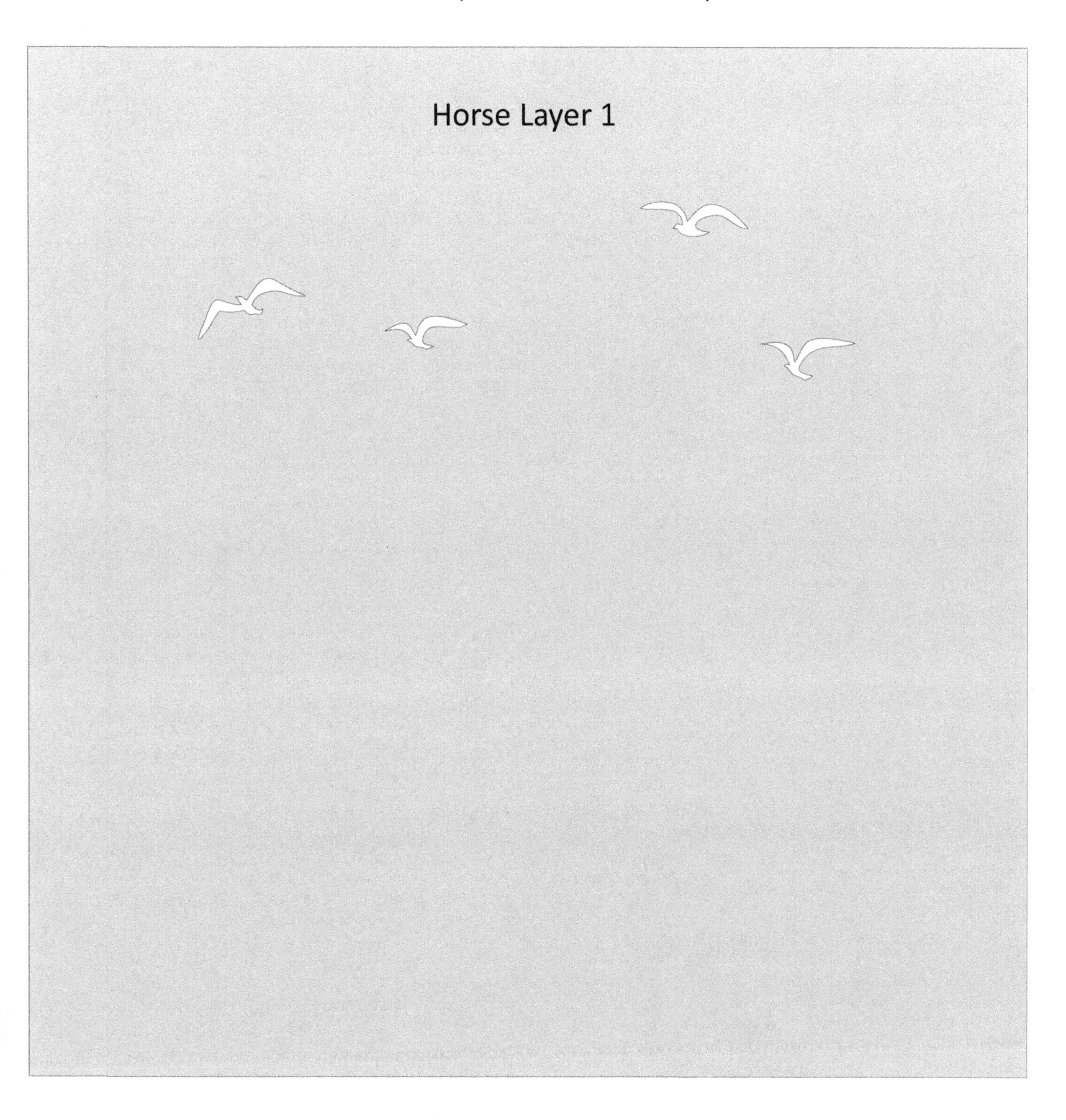

This Page is Intentionally Left blank.

Horse Layer 2

This Page is Intentionally Left blank.

Horse Layer 3

This Page is Intentionally Left blank.

Horse Layer 4

This Page is Intentionally Left blank.

Light house (4 layers)

Size: 7.5 x 7.5 inches or 19x19 cm

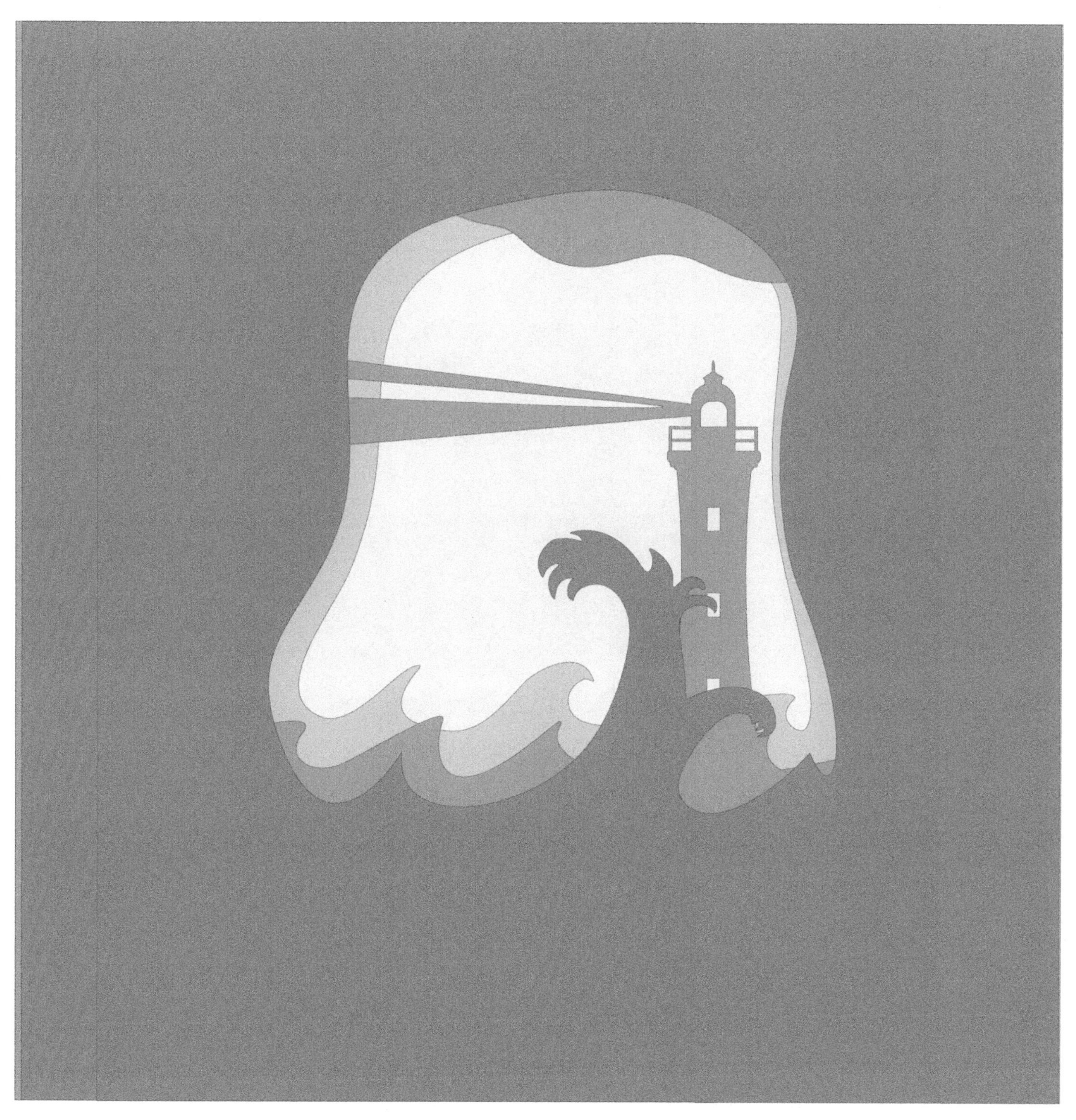

This Page is Intentionally Left blank.

Light House Layer 1

This Page is Intentionally Left blank.

Light House Layer 2

This Page is Intentionally Left blank.

The Details of the light and the light house are optional to cut out or to paint

This Page is Intentionally Left blank.

Light House Layer 4

This Page is Intentionally Left blank.

Ocean (6 layers)

Size: 7.5 x 7.5 inches or 19x19 cm

This Page is Intentionally Left blank.

Ocean Layer 1

This Page is Intentionally Left blank.

Ocean Layer 2

This Page is Intentionally Left blank.

Ocean Layer 3

This Page is Intentionally Left blank.

Ocean Layer 4

This Page is Intentionally Left blank.

Ocean Layer 5

This Page is Intentionally Left blank.

Ocean Layer 6

This Page is Intentionally Left blank.

Deer in the forest (4 layers)

Size 7.5 x7.5 inch or 19x19 cm

The inner details of the deer and the trees in layer 4 are guides to color or if you choose can be cut-out only if you use a hard enough wood or enlarged the .

This Page is Intentionally Left blank.

Deer Layer 1

This Page is Intentionally Left blank.

Deer Layer 2

This Page is Intentionally Left blank.

Deer Layer 3

This Page is Intentionally Left blank.

The Details inside the deer and the trees
are optional to cut out or to paint

This Page is Intentionally Left blank.

House in the forest (4 layers)

Size: 7.25 inches x 9 inches or 18.41 cm x 23 cm

This Page is Intentionally Left blank.

House Layer 1

This Page is Intentionally Left blank.

House Layer 2

This Page is Intentionally Left blank.

House Layer 3

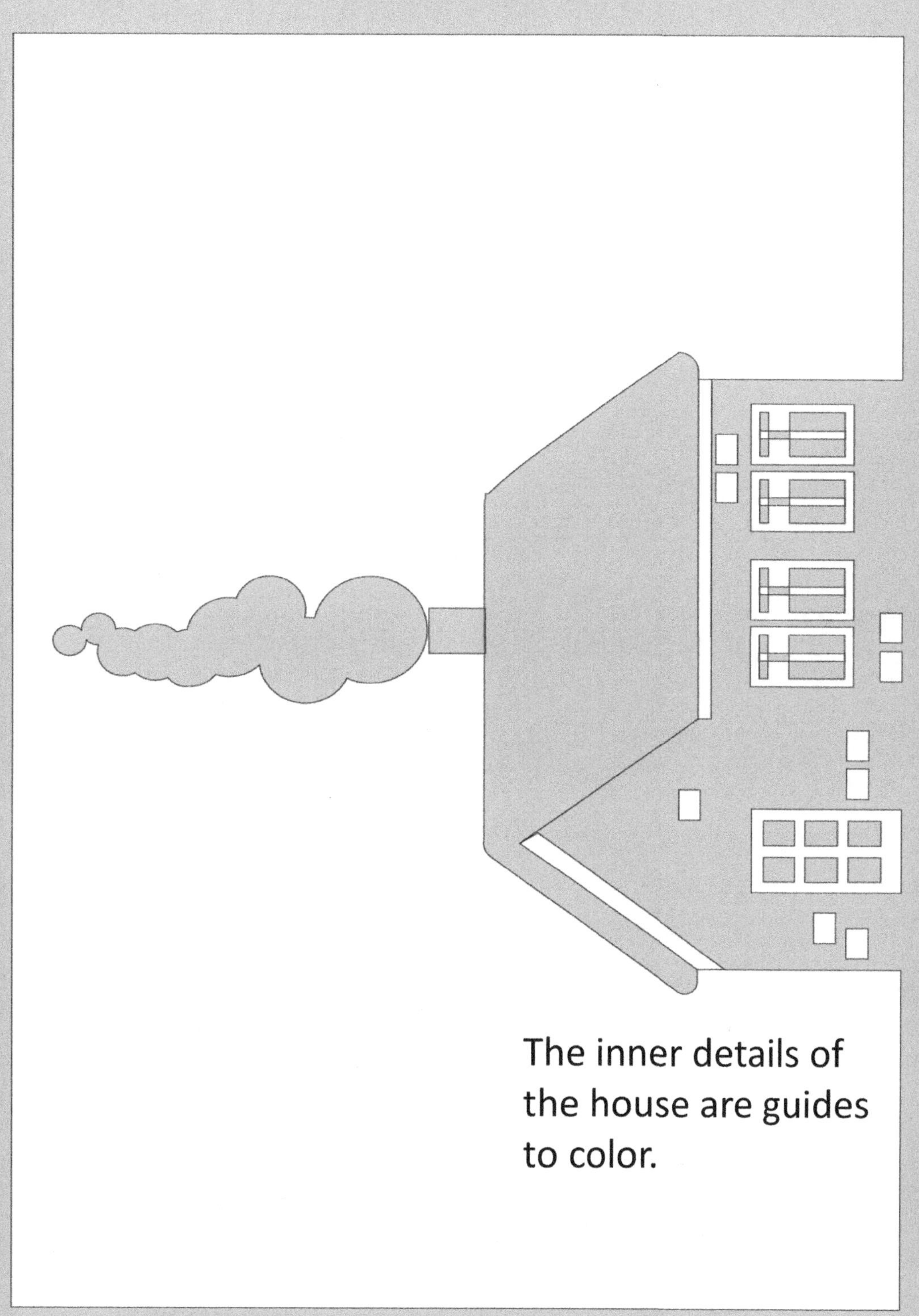

The inner details of the house are guides to color.

This Page is Intentionally Left blank.

House Layer 4

This Page is Intentionally Left blank.

Nature scene (7 layers)

Size: 7.25 inches x 9 inches or 18.41 cm x 23 cm

This Page is Intentionally Left blank.

Nature Scene Layer 1

This Page is Intentionally Left blank.

Nature Scene Layer 2

This Page is Intentionally Left blank.

Nature Scene Layer 3

This Page is Intentionally Left blank.

Nature Scene Layer 4

This Page is Intentionally Left blank.

Nature Scene Layer 5

This Page is Intentionally Left blank.

Nature Scene Layer 6

This Page is Intentionally Left blank.

Nature Scene Layer 7

This Page is Intentionally Left blank.

Hiking (4 layers)

Size: 7.25 inches x 9 inches or 18.41 cm x 23 cm

This Page is Intentionally Left blank.

Hiking Layer 1

This Page is Intentionally Left blank.

Hiking Layer 2

This Page is Intentionally Left blank.

Hiking Layer 3

This Page is Intentionally Left blank.

Hiking Layer 4

This Page is Intentionally Left blank.

Mermaid (5 layers)

Size: 7.25 inches x 9 inches or 18.41 cm x 23 cm

This Page is Intentionally Left blank.

Mermaid Layer 1

The Details are optional to cut out or to paint

This Page is Intentionally Left blank.

Mermaid Layer 2

This Page is Intentionally Left blank.

Mermaid Layer 3

This Page is Intentionally Left blank.

Mermaid Layer 4

This Page is Intentionally Left blank.

Mermaid Layer 5

This Page is Intentionally Left blank.

Cowboy (4 layers)
Size: 7.25 inches x 10 inches or
18.41 cm x 25.4 cm

This Page is Intentionally Left blank.

Cowboy Layer 1

This Page is Intentionally Left blank.

Cowboy Layer 2

This Page is Intentionally Left blank.

Cowboy Layer 3

This Page is Intentionally Left blank.

Cowboy Layer 4

This Page is Intentionally Left blank.

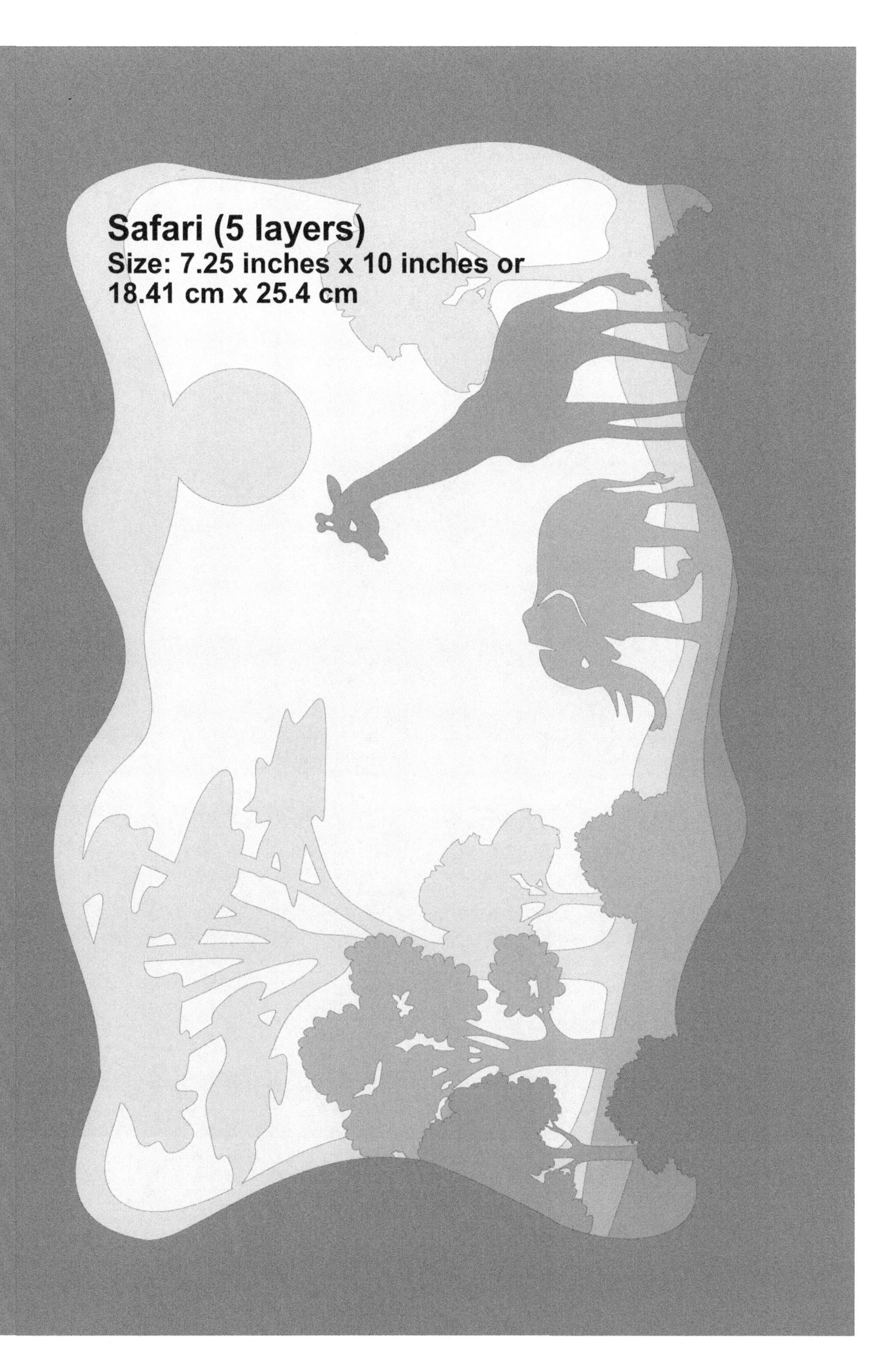
Safari (5 layers)
Size: 7.25 inches x 10 inches or
18.41 cm x 25.4 cm

This Page is Intentionally Left blank.

Safari Layer 1

This Page is Intentionally Left blank.

Safari Layer 2

This Page is Intentionally Left blank.

Safari Layer 3

This Page is Intentionally Left blank.

Safari Layer 4

This Page is Intentionally Left blank.

Safari Layer 5

This Page is Intentionally Left blank.

Swan
(5 layers)
Size:
7 inches x 10 inches or
17.78 cm x 25.4 cm

This Page is Intentionally Left blank.

Swan Layer 1

This Page is Intentionally Left blank.

Swan Layer 2

This Page is Intentionally Left blank.

Swan Layer 3

This Page is Intentionally Left blank.

Swan Layer 4

This Page is Intentionally Left blank.

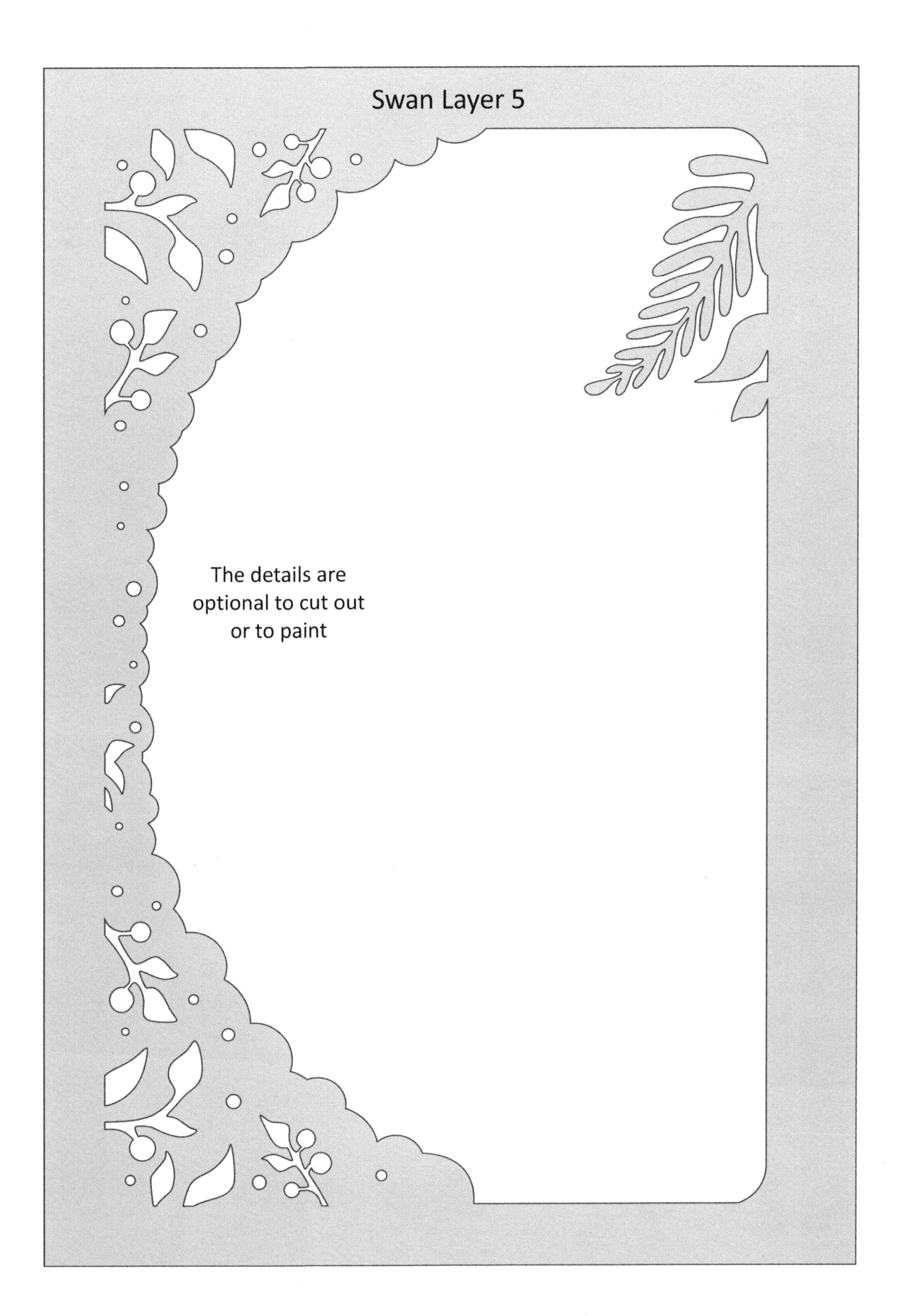
Swan Layer 5
The details are
optional to cut out
or to paint

This Page is Intentionally Left blank.

Made in the USA
Las Vegas, NV
06 January 2025